fast thinking: going to a meeting

PEARSON EDUCATION LIMITED
Head Office:
Edinburgh Gate
Harlow CM20 2JE
Tel: +44 (0)1279 623623
Fax: +44 (0)1279 431059

London Office:
128 Long Acre
London WC2E 9AN
Tel: +44 (0)20 7447 2000
Fax: +44 (0)20 7240 5771
Website: www.fast-thinking.com

First published in Great Britain in 2001

© Pearson Education Limited 2001

The right of Ros Jay to be identified as Author
of this Work has been asserted by him in accordance
with the Copyright, Designs and Patents Act 1988.

ISBN 0 273 65652 X

British Library Cataloguing in Publication Data
A CIP catalogue record for this book can be obtained from the British Library

All rights reserved; no part of this publication may be reproduced, stored
in a retrieval system, or transmitted in any form or by any means, electronic,
mechanical, photocopying, recording, or otherwise without either the prior
written permission of the Publishers or a licence permitting restricted copying
in the United Kingdom issued by the Copyright Licensing Agency Ltd,
90 Tottenham Court Road, London W1P 0LP. This book may not be lent,
resold, hired out or otherwise disposed of by way of trade in any form
of binding or cover other than that in which it is published, without the
prior consent of the Publishers.

10 9 8 7 6 5 4 3 2 1

Typeset by Pantek Arts Ltd, Maidstone, Kent
Printed and bound in Great Britain by Ashford Colour Press, Hampshire

The Publishers' policy is to use paper manufactured from sustainable forests.

fast thinking: going to a meeting

- **influence the discussion**
- **make your point**
- **get the right result**

by Ros Jay

contents

introduction	6
fast thinking gambles	10
1 your objective	12
Negative objectives	13
The subtext of meetings	14
2 before the meeting	18
Influencing the agenda	18
Talking to other people	22
Preparing your case	26
Any other business	29
3 getting your point across	34
Position	35
Problem	37
Possibilities	37
Proposal	38
Winning in debate	41
Don't get emotional	41
Praise other people's contributions	42
And what if you still lose?	43
4 difficult colleagues	46
The role of the chairperson	47
The principles	48

Staying calm	48
Assertiveness	50
The difficult types	51
The rabbiter	51
The pessimist	52
The bully	53
The dominating type	54
The put-down merchant	55

5 chairperson problems 58
The meeting overruns	59
The discussion isn't kept under control	62
Decisions are rushed	63
The chairperson controls all the decisions	64

6 coping with conflict 68
The causes of conflict	68
Status battles	70
Be pleasant	71
Practice win/win negotiating	71
Any other business	72
Turf wars	74
Dealing with anger	75

7 types of meeting 80
Departmental meetings	81
Inter-departmental meetings	82
Project meetings	84
External meetings	85

going to a meeting in 15 minutes 88

introduction

Another bloody meeting to go to. And you've only got 15 minutes to get your head around it. Why are you dreading this one? Maybe you know you're going to end up having a row with Alex from accounts over the late payers policy. Or they're bound to veto your request for extra staff for the exhibition. Or is Pat going to make you feel small and pathetic again? Maybe you just know it'll waste half a day and achieve nothing, and you simply haven't got time for it. And what's more, you haven't even had time to prepare for it.

Meetings take up a huge part of our working lives, but when life's already too short to cram everything in, how are you supposed to justify the time they take? Especially if they end up causing conflict and you never get what you want from them anyway. The answer is, you have to make them work for you. What you need is fast thinking to prepare quickly, get what you want from the meeting, and minimise conflict. And above all, you want to come out of your meetings looking good. If every meeting achieves a worthwhile result, earns you respect, and makes your bosses sit up and notice you … well, you won't be wasting your time any more, will you?

This is about how to prepare quickly for a meeting when all that time you'd scheduled for preparation has mysteriously vanished. And about how to make all the meetings you attend more beneficial for you without taking up any more of your time. In fact, this book is full of tips on how to save time at meetings.

Ideally, you should put aside some time to prepare for important meetings. But who lives in an ideal world these days? No, what you need is:

 tips for looking as if you know more than you do

 shortcuts for doing as little preparation as possible

 checklists to make sure you've got everything covered

… all put together clearly and simply. And short enough to read fast, of course.

Suppose you have an evening – maybe longer if you're lucky – to prepare for an important meeting. Perhaps it's the initial meeting for a big project, or maybe you're going to introduce an

This is about how to prepare quickly for a meeting when all that time you'd scheduled for preparation has mysteriously vanished

important proposal in front of several senior colleagues. Or perhaps you need to prepare a strong case to argue against someone else's proposal. This book will tell you everything you need to know to prepare for the meeting, to win your case, and to look good with it. Oh, and if you've somehow left yourself only 15 minutes to get ready (how did that happen?) you'll even find a section at the end of the book just for you.

So don't panic even if you've left things late. By the time you've read this book you'll know how to wrap the meeting round your little finger, and get whatever you want from it. It's all a matter of knowing how to think fast and act smart. The techniques are all in here, and they're all simple to master once you know how.

work at the speed of life

This book will take you through the key skills you need to master to get the most from the meetings you attend:

1. The first thing to do is to decide what your objective is for this meeting, and for all your meetings.
2. Before the meeting you need to prepare for the important agenda items, and research any information which will back up your case. You may also want to influence the agenda, and the earlier you attempt to do

this the more success you are likely to have.

3. If you have an important case to put at the meeting – with not necessarily a lot of time to express it – you'll need to prepare it well and argue it clearly, succinctly and persuasively.

4. Some colleagues can be tough to deal with at meetings. Maybe they always put you down, or perhaps they pooh-pooh every idea. They may not even be aware that they are making your life harder, but they still need to be dealt with effectively.

5. What are you supposed to do if you're stuck in a badly chaired meeting? Chapter 5 will tell you what you can do to speed things up and help the meeting run more efficiently and effectively, even when you're not the one in charge.

6. One of the most unpleasant – and sadly too frequent – features of many meetings is conflict. Not just polite disagreement, but heated and angry arguments. These do you no good at all, so Chapter 6 will fill you in on how to keep the temperature down, and get what you want too.

7. There are plenty of different kinds of meeting, and while most of the guidelines apply to all of them, Chapter 7 will give you a few specific tips for getting the most from each type.

8. Finally, just in case you like to sail really close to the wind (or maybe don't like to but find you've done it anyway), you'll find a crash course in preparing for a meeting in 15 minutes.

By the time you've read this book you'll know how to wrap the meeting round your little finger, and get whatever you want from it

fast thinking gambles

No one is suggesting that you should spend an hour preparing for every weekly departmental meeting, or every fortnightly project review meeting. But some meetings really are important. Crucial decisions will be made which you want to influence; your own ideas and proposals will be challenged by other people. These meetings are worth preparing for thoroughly. That might mean half an hour, or it might mean half a day's research finding the facts to back up your case. Or a couple of hours briefing other people or planning a joint argument.

If you leave your planning to the last minute for these important meetings, you can still get by with the fast thinking techniques in this book. But it's bound to be a gamble. There's always the risk that your lack of preparation will show, or that you'll lose a debate you might have won with more preparation time:

- You may strongly disagree with someone at the meeting, but be unable to produce the facts you need to back up your argument.

- Someone may challenge you and find the gaps in your scantily prepared case. They may ask questions you should be able to answer but can't.

- You may be caught on the hop with a point for a decision you wanted to influence but haven't the information you need.

- The mood of the meeting might not be what you'd banked on – a few conversations in advance could have forewarned you how strong the opposition would be, or what their main arguments would be.

- You may find yourself getting into a heated row and looking weak, when careful preparation could have meant you'd have kept your cool and come out on top.

So taking time to prepare for an important meeting is well worth it … next time. But you don't want to hear that now. You just want to know how to get the results you want at short notice. OK, fair enough; it's all here. And once you've got the hang of it, you'll know how to invest that extra time you're going to leave in the future to maximum effect.

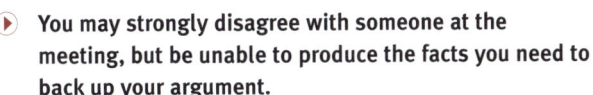

No one is suggesting that you should spend an hour preparing for every weekly departmental meeting, or every fortnightly project review meeting

1 your objective

An hour or less to your meeting and you're supposed to start setting objectives? Wasn't this book supposed to be about doing things fast, not messing about with boring management theory? Yes, quite right. This *is* about doing things fast. It's also about doing them effectively. And you can't get the most out of your meeting until you know what it is you want out of it.

In fact, when it comes to meetings, your objectives will apply to individual agenda items – unless the whole meeting is about a single issue. So you need to go through the agenda and identify what it is you want from each item. Your objectives might include the following:

- **To ensure that a particular decision is made.**
- **To ensure that a particular decision is avoided.**
- **To ensure that any decision reached doesn't put extra strain on the budget, overstretch staff, transfer authority out of the department, or whatever.**

- **To delay a decision being made (perhaps until you've found time to do more research).**
- **To ensure that certain action points are allocated to you.**
- **To ensure that certain action points are *not* allocated to you.**
- **To ensure that action is taken on the agenda item in question, and the item isn't stalled.**

Note down your objective for each item, so that during the meeting you stay focused on what you really want. You're trying to keep this meeting moving as fast as it can, so you won't want to waste your time on sidelines or digressions from the main point. You'll need to keep all your contributions focused on the objective you want to achieve for the item being discussed.

Negative objectives

This process is worthwhile because the objective isn't always as obvious as you think. You might think that your aim is to achieve a particular decision when, in fact, what's really important is simply to *avoid* some other decision. It might not be the end of the world if your proposal isn't accepted, so long as Jack's isn't accepted either. This is where negative objectives come in: *To prevent a decision which*

> You need to go through the agenda and identify what it is you want from each item

entails more paperwork for my team is a perfectly valid objective.

It should go without saying that you do not need to identify objectives for items such as 'date of next meeting' (except perhaps to make sure you can attend) or 'apologies for absence'.

THE SUBTEXT OF MEETINGS

So much for setting objectives. But you also need to be aware of what really goes on at meetings – and especially at important meetings. They are the place where people battle it out for status, and advertise themselves for promotion, hoping they

PASS

If you're going through this process in a hurry, you can save time by identifying your objectives for only the most important agenda items. If you're not that bothered about how many car parking spaces are allocated to directors, or whether the cafeteria should open half an hour earlier in the mornings, skip setting objectives for these items. But make sure you know what your objective is for the items that matter to you.

can make themselves stand out from the crowd. Nobody admits this openly, but they're all doing it.

And with good reason. Meetings really are the best forum for exhibiting your talents. Promotions – especially high-flying ones – are rarely decided on performance. In fact, good performance in your job is a very good reason for leaving you in it. No, most key promotions are earned with a particularly brilliant report, an impressive presentation, or outstanding performance at meetings. These are the things that make your bosses, and your bosses' bosses, notice you and single you out as a high achiever.

So every meeting which is attended by people who can further your career is an opportunity to show that you are a succinct and intelligent thinker who can handle people effectively and put across strong and convincing arguments. If you waffle, ramble, get emotional, use ill-prepared arguments, or let it show that you haven't done your homework properly, you not only fail to meet your immediate objectives for the agenda, you also damage your career prospects.

You need to know this not only because it is crucial to your career, but also because everybody else at the meeting knows it. However, not all of

> Most key promotions are earned with a particularly brilliant report, an impressive presentation, or outstanding performance at meetings

them know how best to impress their bosses. So once you know the techniques for looking good at meetings – which is all part of how to get what you want from them – you'll find that you have the edge over your colleagues and you have every chance of getting noticed by the people who count.

for next time

Go through the agenda *as soon as you receive it* and set an objective for each item. You need to do this as early as possible because your objective may indicate something else that needs to be done. You might need to research some facts to present at the meeting to ensure you meet your objective, or enlist support from colleagues, or ask the chairperson to add or remove agenda items (we'll be looking at all these things in the next chapter).

None of these things are simple – and some are downright impossible – if you don't set your objectives until the last minute. The longer you give yourself to do it, the more chance you have of ensuring that you actually meet the objectives. And, what's more, you'll save yourself this last-minute rush another time.

Once you know the techniques for looking good at meetings you'll find that you have the edge over your colleagues

2 before the meeting

Given enough time, there's plenty you can usefully do before the meeting to make it work better for you. OK, you haven't got enough time – not this time. But you can still do plenty. And you won't need to do everything in this chapter every time. What you do will be determined by the items on the agenda.

The preparation you can do falls into three categories:

- influencing the agenda
- talking to other people
- preparing your case.

INFLUENCING THE AGENDA

How often have you looked at an agenda (whether early on or at the last moment) and thought:

- 'Oh, no. I don't want that discussed yet. I need to get those figures out of Jim first, and he's on holiday for another week.'

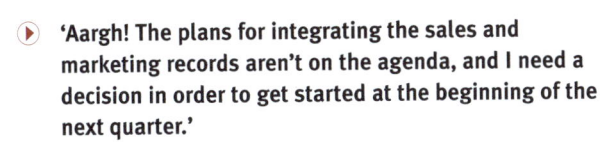

- 'Aargh! The plans for integrating the sales and marketing records aren't on the agenda, and I need a decision in order to get started at the beginning of the next quarter.'
- 'Oh. Item 8 is for decision but surely we can't make a decision until we've collected more information?'
- 'How on earth are we supposed to discuss item 3 with Pauline on holiday? Her input is essential or we'll never stop Mike doing it his way – which will never work.'
- 'This is crazy! Why discuss staffing plans *before* we finalise the budget? The budget will partly determine the staffing levels.'
- 'Oh, no! I wanted to discuss the outline plan for the office move, but I haven't had a chance to do all the preparation for discussing the finer details.'

… And so on. All of these are agendas which make it harder for you to do your job, or get what you want from the meeting. Items there which you don't want to have to discuss yet (and not just because you haven't left time to prepare); items *not* there which you need a decision on; broad topics for discussion which you are ready only to discuss certain aspects of; items ordered illogically which will at best waste time, and at worst lead to ill-informed decisions.

So what can you do? You can try to get the agenda changed, that's what. And the best time to

> You won't need to do everything in this chapter every time. What you do will be determined by the items on the agenda

do this (you'll love this one) is before it's written. Sounds daft, I know, but look at it from the point of view of the chairperson. If they agree to change an agenda item after the agenda's been circulated, that's more work for them. And if they do it for you, everyone else will be on to them to make alterations. They don't want to show favouritism, so do they do it for eveyone else, too? And if they get a reputation for being a soft touch when it comes to rewriting agendas, they'll have to rework every one they do. That means extra work for them, and no one's ever sure when they've got the final version.

thinking smart

FOR THE GREATER GOOD

If you really want to influence the agenda after it's been circulated, you'll need to give the chairperson a very good reason for letting you do so: a reason they can confidently use to explain why they're not making changes for anyone else. So make it sound as if the change isn't for your benefit, but for the benefit of the meeting. 'I'm worried that the meeting won't be informed well enough to make the right decision if Pauline's not there to contribute,' rather than, 'I'll never be able to put my case against Mike without Pauline's support. It's not fair!'

What would you do in their shoes? Refuse to alter agendas after they'd been circulated, if you had any sense. And that's why you need to influence them in advance if you possibly can. So anticipate what will and won't be included. Make a note during meetings to remind you if the chairperson says that they'll include a particular item on the agenda for next time. And think about what's likely to be included.

Then it's simple to give the chairperson a quick ring before they write it (if you don't know how far ahead they usually work, contact them within a couple of days of the meeting being scheduled). Ask for a quick word about the agenda, and mention any items you want included or are concerned about. Say, 'I take it we'll be discussing the budget before we make a decision on the staffing?' or, 'I wonder if the details of the office move won't take too long to discuss in full? Could I suggest that we decide the outline plan for now, and set up a separate meeting to discuss the details?' and so on. Make sure you sound deferential, and you will not only get the influence you want (so long as you can present a good case for each request), but you will also impress the chairperson with your forethought and preparation.

You will not only get the influence you want but you will also impress the chairperson with your forethought and preparation

11 — thinking fast

KEEP IT PRIVATE

If you have to ask for last-minute changes to the agenda – like now, when you've only just looked at it – call the chairperson privately a few minutes before the meeting. Don't try to collar them after they've arrived. They'll be more receptive in private, and there's no danger of anyone else overhearing and arguing against you. Give them convincing reasons for making changes, or you've got no chance.

TALKING TO OTHER PEOPLE

The agenda's been settled – with or without your intervention – but there's still work you can do to influence the success of the meeting. And one of the key things you can do is talk to other people. And how does this help? Well, in a number of ways:

To find out their attitude to specific issues. It helps to know whether all of the half dozen people in the meeting are going to agree with you or disagree, or what the split will be. There's no point spending hours preparing an argument if it turns out everyone agrees with you anyway. But there's a lot of point if you're going to be heavily outnumbered. And, of course, it's not just down to numbers. It makes a big difference which people are or aren't on your side. So sound out the other members of the meeting – at least the most influential ones – so you know what you're up against.

If you talk to people in advance of the meeting to find out who is and isn't in agreement with you, it will also help if you can find out what the arguments against you are. So if a colleague tells you, 'Actually, I'm dead against relocating the Essex office and moving them onto this site with us,' ask them what their reasons are. You don't have to say you're preparing your case for the meeting – you're simply asking their view on a current issue. You may not even have to tell them you disagree – you could indicate that you're still deciding what you think is best.

To solicit their support. If you can enlist your colleagues' support before the meeting, you know you won't be alone in arguing your case. So talk to any likely prospects – take them for a lunchtime drink or a bite of lunch if there's time – and get them on board.

To share resources. You and your colleagues haven't got a lot of spare time even when you prepare in advance. So why spend hours doing all the research you need to back up your case alone?

> There's no point spending hours preparing an argument if it turns out everyone agrees with you anyway. But there's a lot of point if you're going to be heavily outnumbered

Get those colleagues who agree with your side of the argument to share out the preparation work — one of you find out the prices of alternative options from the one being proposed, one of you go online to find relevant statistics, one of you talk to the staff to find out what their views are, one of you dig out that article from last month's issue of *Business Week*, and so on.

Just make sure you don't rely on unreliable colleagues for essential information. You'll need to get together before the meeting to pool your resources and check your facts don't contradict each other or undermine your argument. But if you've cut things fine you can divvy up the work as little as half an hour before the meeting and share the results 10 minutes before it starts. Clearly, more time than this is preferable if you can manage it.

 thinking smart

PRESERVING LOYALTY

If you've persuaded someone round to supporting you at the meeting and you want to consolidate their support, ask them to help research the facts to back up the case. It will make it much harder for them to change sides when it comes to the meeting.

To find out information you need to present your case effectively. Colleagues who are attending the meeting are not the only people you may need to talk to. It can lend huge weight to your case to be able to say, 'I've sounded out a few of our suppliers about this …' or, 'I've talked to three of our other regional accounts managers to find out how they handle this …' or, 'We've run a mini-survey among the staff in the transport department and they feel …' So talk to anyone you can think of whose opinion or experience will lend support and credibility to your argument. Even if you're so pressed for time that you have only five minutes to spare before the meeting, a quick phone call to the right person can be a big help.

If this all sounds like a huge amount of work in the time you've got (if indeed you've got any time at all), bear in mind that you're not likely to have to do this for every agenda item. There may be only one controversial item on the agenda – or at least only one that you are particularly concerned about. And you may not need to research any background facts on it. Or perhaps you don't need to speak to other people about it – suppliers, customers, staff and so on. Some meetings require very little preparation time, although some are

'It can lend huge weight to your case to be able to say, 'I've sounded out a few of our suppliers about this …''

important and complex enough that you may want to put hours or even days into getting your preparation absolutely right.

PREPARING YOUR CASE

It doesn't matter how little time you've got, this is the place to invest it. The next chapter is all about how to put your point across effectively, but you can't do that without facts and figures to back it up. So find them. It helps tremendously to have some idea of the arguments that will be levelled against you; that way, with limited time, you can direct your research where it is most useful.

thinking smart
DON'T RUN WITH THE CROWD
Remember that meetings are places to impress, as well as to get your point across. So dig up some information on key agenda items even if they're not controversial. Come up with facts (just one useful fact for one agenda item will do) that no one else has found. Don't pull data out of the accompanying papers that everyone has. Talk to an expert for two minutes, or go online and find some relevant statistics. Then impress everyone with information that only you have bothered – or thought – to unearth.

The best way to decide what research needs doing is to list the key arguments you want to make in your favour. There will generally be up to about half a dozen of these. Suppose the issue in question is whether to relocate to larger offices, and you are opposed to the plan. Your arguments might be:

- **huge upheaval resulting in a drop in productivity for several weeks**
- **staff are opposed to the idea**
- **no available site as convenient as this**
- **move is unnecessary.**

Now you want to think about the most convincing facts you could come up with to support each of these arguments, and then go and dig out the facts:

- *Huge upheaval resulting in low productivity.* **Talk to other organisations or branches of your company which have relocated, and ask for their experiences, especially any figures on productivity during the move, and how long the effects lasted. Look for similar data on the Internet or in the trade press.**

The best way to decide what research needs doing is to list the key arguments you want to make in your favour

- *Staff opposed to the idea.* Talk to the staff, or the managers concerned. Run a mini-poll if you can. Dig out letters or articles in staff publications. Get input from trade union reps.
- *No other site as convenient.* Compare this site with proposed locations for proximity to rail stations and main roads, convenience for staff, ease of recruiting staff, access for transport fleet, rush-hour traffic flows and so on.
- *Move is unnecessary.* Find alternatives to avoid overcrowding present site. For example, demonstrate how certain departments could operate from their own site without posing communication problems, or how present site could be utilised more effectively. Perhaps talk to specialist architect or planner.

You get the picture. Decide what data will best support your argument, and then find it. The second stage of the process is to list the opposition's key arguments, and repeat the process for these, looking for data to refute the arguments. For example:

- Present site is overcrowded.
- A purpose-built site will be more cost-effective to run.
- Current offices are shabby and run-down, and a new building will present a far better image for the organisation.

In the first instance, as you can see, you have already done the research. But the second and third arguments raise points which you can usefully dig out more facts and figures on. For example, the cost of refurbishing the present buildings, or the ease of introducing more cost-effective practices at the existing site.

So to prepare your case, you must establish which facts and figures will most usefully:

1. **support your case**
2. **refute the case for the opposition.**

Then spend whatever time you have (even if it's not much) finding the information you need. If time is really tight, just concentrate on backing up the one or two key arguments. If you need more advice on how to research the information you need, have a look at *fast thinking: finding facts*.

ANY OTHER BUSINESS

The best chairpeople don't include 'any other business' on their agenda. You can always add vital and urgent items at the last minute if you have to, but 'any other business' is an invitation to the meeting not only to waste time but also to exercise

> 'Any other business' is an invitation to the meeting not only to waste time but also to exercise more Machiavellian practices

thinking fast

THE ULTIMATE TOOL

If time is really tight – and sometimes even if it's not – you may be able to use the ultimate fast thinking technique for saving time at meetings: don't go. Clearly you can only do this if there are no agenda items you want to influence the outcome of – but then that's often the case. Always contact the chairperson and ask permission (the earlier the better, but let's not get picky this time). You may be able to ask for one or two points to be made on your behalf, or to offer a couple of relevant facts the meeting might find useful, but keep this to a minimum. Otherwise it will sound as if you really ought to be there.

---

more Machiavellian practices. Underhand and sly members of the meeting like to use the opportunity to discuss a subject for which no one else has prepared, having been unaware it would arise. Obviously they do this when they expect opposition and want to catch their opponents on the hop.

So what do you do if your chairperson does include 'any other business' on the agenda? We'll look later at techniques for persuading them not to allow people to raise such items, but your best tactic is to be prepared. Consider whether there are any topics likely to be raised to catch you off guard. Is there a particular bone of contention at the moment which isn't scheduled to be discussed this time? Your opponent may generate some excuse to discuss it now rather than later. Or they may raise some loosely related issue because it will help their cause later on.

For example, the real, ongoing issue may be whether or not the company should attend a big exhibition at the NEC next year. One of your colleagues is opposed, while you – and perhaps other colleagues too – are in favour. So your opponent introduces a last-minute item under 'any other business' asking for agreement to take part in some other event 'in late spring next year' for which they need to book urgently (their excuse for raising it under 'aob'). Only after the meeting has agreed, and the booking been made, do you discover that the event in question clashes with the exhibition. Staff will be so stretched that your case for attending the exhibition has been weakened.

Obviously, you can't be ready for every shifty move your opponents might make. But you can prepare your case for attending the exhibition early, knowing that they may well try to bring the discussion forward and catch you off guard. Well,

The best chairpeople don't include 'any other business' on their agenda

thinking fast

LOOKING GOOD

Are you really pressed for time, but need to look as if you've done your homework? Scribble a few notes in light pencil on the agenda (light so no one else can read them). Dot random post-it notes through reports you should have read. Highlight the occasional phrase or point in the papers that accompanied the agenda – just pick them at whim. Your colleagues will be amazed at the thoroughness with which you have evidently studied your paperwork.

you won't be off guard. Not only will you recognise the ploy to book the other event for what it is, but when you therefore pin your opponent down on dates, and they turn it into a discussion about the exhibition, you'll be ready with your facts and your arguments.

One of the joys of this is that your opponent, thinking you'll be entirely unprepared yourself, may well not have thought it necessary to prepare as thoroughly as you have. I believe that's what is known as being 'hoisted by their own petard'.

So the moral is, as soon as you know there's a contentious subject in the offing that you feel strongly about, get your argument ready and take the relevant papers to every meeting at which it could be raised. You're bound to need it eventually – the preparation is hardly going to be wasted – and in the meantime no one's going to spring any surprises on you.

for next time

The longer you have, the more time you can invest in making sure the meeting goes the way you want it to. So in future, as soon as you have a meeting date set, schedule time in your diary several days in advance to start your preparations. You may not need long, but you need it ahead of time, not at the last minute. It takes time to get hold of people, and the results of any research you do may take time to come back.

And remember that the earlier you talk to the chairperson about any changes you want to make to the agenda, the more likely they are to cooperate. If you can, talk to them before the agenda is written and circulated.

As soon as you know there's a contentious subject in the offing that you feel strongly about, get your argument ready and take the relevant papers to every meeting

3 getting your point across

You may have a valid case to put – possibly one that you feel is compelling – but somehow your colleagues don't always see it the same way. In fact, they sometimes barely let you express it at all. So how can you make the most of whatever time you are allotted, and be sure of making the most convincing case possible, with everyone actually listening to you?

As always, preparation is important. You may not get a chance to repeat yourself, and you may not get long to speak. So you need to be:

- clear
- succinct.

If you decide in advance what you want to say, you are far more likely to achieve these two objectives. So what you want is a simple formula for expressing yourself clearly and briefly. And, as luck would have it, I've got just the formula you need.

What you need to do is to compress the points you want to make into a kind of mini-presentation. It might take as little as 20 or 30 seconds, and have a relatively informal feel, but it should still follow the format of a presentation. After all, presentations are designed to put across an argument persuasively and with clarity, which is exactly what you are aiming for here.

So here's the formula around which to prepare what you'll be saying:

1. **position**
2. **problem**
3. **possibilities**
4. **proposal**

… a simple four-step process which you can apply to any argument you want to express at a meeting.

POSITION

You need to start by clarifying the situation. This may take only half a sentence, but it is worth doing. Suppose the issue is over whether or not to move offices. You might start by saying, 'At the moment, the entire South West regional staff is based here

How can you make the most of whatever time you are allotted, and be sure of making the most convincing case possible, with everyone actually listening to you?

thinking smart

BOOK YOUR PLACE

If you're worried that you may not get a word in edgewise at this meeting – too many other people there who like the sound of their own voice – have a word with the chairperson before the meeting and say, for example, 'I've been doing some research into item 4 on the agenda, which I think will be very helpful to the meeting. Could you please see that I get a chance to outline it?'

at this site…' You may feel you're stating the obvious, but it has several advantages:

- **There may be people at the meeting for whom this is a new topic, and the basic facts may not be as obvious to everyone as you might think.**

- **This is the first step of expressing the issue in a nutshell. Encapsulating the whole issue for everyone in the space of a few sentences generates clarity – especially if the meeting has been talking round the issue and disappearing down related sidetracks for some time. And it shows that you are one of those people who can step back and look at the big picture, something which will do your reputation no harm at all.**

- However much disagreement there has been until now, your opening couple of sentences will promote unity. You're all agreed what the position is – the debate is over what to do about it. It never hurts to get everyone to agree with you, even if it only lasts until you hit the controversial points.

- Just occasionally, there will be disagreement in the meeting over what the real issue or problem is. Summarising it like this should bring any confusion out into the open and allow it to be resolved in order to tackle the real problem effectively.

Problem

Now it's time to go on and state why the current position won't do – why it needs to be addressed. For example, 'As the organisation grows, it's becoming increasingly difficult to fit everyone on to this site.' You're phrasing the problem in a way that everyone can agree with, but which maintains clarity and continues summarising the issue in a nutshell.

Possibilities

You want to carry on being as uncontroversial as possible here, to maintain agreement and to deter interruptions. One important component of this is to sound as impartial as possible. This is an advantage because:

You need to start by clarifying the situation. This may take only half a sentence, but it is worth doing

- It encourages everyone else to listen rather than argue, as they would with a biased or emotive statement.

- It makes you sound like the kind of balanced, rational person who can see all the sides of an argument. Not only will this impress your colleagues and superiors, but it also lends credibility to your proposed solution – it will be the proposal of someone who has weighed up all the facts logically, not someone who has barged in with a reflex emotional response.

- It means you are genuinely contributing a useful, succinct summary of the situation to help the meeting retain its clarity.

So you might summarise the possibilities by saying, 'There are three basic options: we move to a new site; we move *part* of the regional operation to a new site; or we stay here and adapt the present site to cope with the pressures of growth.' There. It's hard to see how anyone could reasonably take issue with that.

Proposal

You've established an oasis of agreement in the midst of your meeting. Now it's time to state which of the possibilities you prefer. Again, you do this very simply, and you give your key arguments (the ones you prepared earlier) to justify your view.

thinking smart

LET ME FINISH …

If you don't want to be interrupted while your speaking, here are two techniques which make it very hard for people to interrupt you without being downright rude:

- State how many points you have to make: 'There are three reasons for this view…' It's hard for people not to let you finish.
- Breathe in mid-sentence, so you don't have to pause for breath at the end. That way, they don't get a look in unless they interrupt you in mid-stream.

These are the key arguments which give you the best chance of achieving your objective for this agenda item (which we discussed in Chapter 1).

For example: 'After looking at the options, I believe the best choice is to stay here for four key reasons. Firstly, my research shows that the upheaval involved in this kind of move tends to lead to an average drop in productivity of 50 per cent, lasting for up to three months. Secondly, the move would be unpopular with the staff, 67 per cent of whom are against it at the moment. Thirdly, this site is ideally located both for commuting access for staff and for key distribution routes. The two main

---

You've established an oasis of agreement in the midst of your meeting. Now it's time to state which of the possibilities you prefer

alternative sites proposed are unpopular with employees – making recruitment harder – and one is in the middle of a particularly notorious rush-hour congestion area. Finally, I have evidence to indicate that this site could be redesigned and refurbished at a lower cost than relocation. My figures show that with sound planning we could accommodate a 4 per cent growth for at least 10 more years without expanding out of this site.'

Was that convincing, or was that convincing? You've been brief, clear and very persuasive. If anyone wants to question you, they'll find you can quote chapter and verse for all the figures you gave. If they try to bring counter-arguments, you've got data to refute those too (you researched it in

thinking smart

SUMMING UP COURAGE

Meetings can be quite intimidating, especially if there are a lot of senior colleagues present, or maybe important customers. So prepare your mini-proposal well, and then ask a friend or colleague to rehearse you, and tell you how persuasive and well thought out it sounds. At worst you'll end up sounding good (which is plenty); at best you'll come across as brilliant.

Chapter 2, remember?). You've got your point across as effectively as you could have wished, and you won't have failed to impress anyone worth impressing in the process.

WINNING IN DEBATE

Once you've made your point initially, you're into the process of reinforcing it through debate and questioning. Or you may be responding to someone else's input. When you're into this stage of the meeting, there are a few tips you will find useful to help you sound convincing and persuasive, and give you the best chance of getting the result you want.

Don't get emotional

However strongly you feel about the issue under discussion, don't allow yourself to become emotional about it. People see emotion and reason as opposites, and the more emotion you display, the less rational you will appear. You want to look like someone whose judgements and opinions are based on logical reasoning. Displays of emotion — especially negative emotions such as fear, anger, sadness and so on — will undermine your credibility and therefore your argument.

> People see emotion and reason as opposites, and the more emotion you display, the less rational you will appear

thinking smart

FOOLS RUSH IN

If there's a round-robin discussion in which everyone takes it in turn to express their view, try to be as close to the last to speak as you can. It gives you a chance to gauge the mood of the meeting, to collect extra facts and data as they are divulged, and to hear the main arguments that you will want to add to or refute. Be brief and succinct and, as the last to speak, yours will be the argument that sticks most firmly in many people's minds.

Praise other people's contributions

You are far more likely to get the result you want from the meeting if you remain pleasant and popular with everyone. If people take agin you for being aggressive, pompous, arrogant, sarcastic, belligerent or anything else, they will be far more reluctant to vote in your favour. So remain friendly no matter what.

One of the best techniques for staying in favour is to praise other people and their contributions to the meeting. And especially, praise them when you are going on to disagree with them. For example, 'Monica is absolutely right to say that employee response is terribly important, and I was impressed that she managed to find so many relevant figures. But I think we have to take into account that many of our staff have only the haziest idea of what is really being proposed …' and so on.

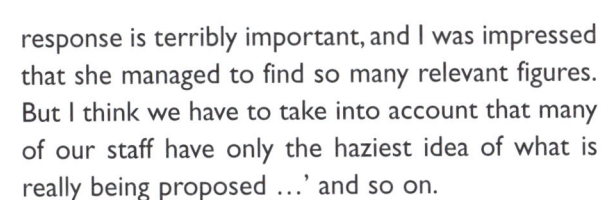

This technique makes you sound magnanimous and ready to acknowledge a good contribution – so when you subsequently disagree it clearly wasn't personal prejudice or sour grapes. The conclusion everyone will have to draw is that your disagreement is based on sound and rational judgement. And the person with whom you have disagreed will take it far less personally if they feel they have also been praised publicly in the process.

Just one word of warning: if you disagree with people a lot, use this technique sparingly or very subtly. If people see it as a ruse rather than as a genuine expression of praise, it will sound very hollow. As a rule of thumb, the more genuine you are in your praise, the more genuine it will sound (no surprises there, but worth bearing in mind).

And what if you still lose?

There will always be times when you don't get the result you want. Even if your case was brilliant, there may be other factors. Office politics and

> The person with whom you have disagreed will take it far less personally if they feel they have also been praised publicly in the process

personal prejudices can prevent the best argument from winning at times. So don't take it personally. Handle it with dignity and good grace, but get your disagreement minuted. This means that when it all falls apart later – just as you predicted it would – you can remind the meeting that you disagreed with the decision all along. You won't be popular if you gloat with a smug 'Told you so!' but a polite reference to your disagreement will remind people that your judgement was sound.

So if the decision goes against you, don't sulk or get upset or angry. Accept it. Say, 'If that's the feeling of the meeting, obviously I'll go along with it. But I still feel we'll encounter problems with low productivity and high costs. I'd be grateful, chairman, if my views could be minuted.' Simple, brief and amicable, but firm about your disagreement.

for next time

Prepare any arguments you care about carefully, and decide how to make your point clearly and briefly, using the format: position, problem, possibilities, proposal. The more facts you can back up your case with, the better. But you don't want to cram them all into your mini-presentation; save all but the key ones for later in the debate.

The more time you give yourself before each meeting, the more agenda items you will be able to prepare a useful and influential input into.

If the decision goes against you, don't sulk or get upset or angry. Accept it

4 difficult colleagues

Some people are a joy to attend meetings with – people like you (at least, once you've read this book). They are positive, they contribute well and succinctly, they encourage other people and they help the meeting run effectively and fast. And then there's the rest of them. I'm not talking about really unpleasant encounters in meetings – we'll be looking at that in Chapter 6. I'm simply talking about people who have character traits that make the meetings they attend more difficult or less fruitful.

These people probably don't even know they're doing it. But you, unfortunately, can't fail to notice. Maybe they always put you and your ideas down, or perhaps they like to dominate the meeting. Maybe they just won't shut up, and you can see your precious time being eaten away to no purpose.

THE ROLE OF THE CHAIRPERSON

It's worth making a point about your chairperson here: except in the case of the most minor infringements of behaviour, a really good chairperson will keep the lid on these problems so you don't need to. The occasional remark such as, 'Let's not get personal,' or, 'It's time to summarise and move on,' or, 'That's a valid criticism, but what do you see as the best points of this proposal?' should ensure that the meeting remains positive, friendly and effective, and runs to schedule. However, not enough chairpeople are this good, so you're going to have to do their job for them.

Of course, a chairperson – however good – can't change people's personalities. They can't turn a whiner into a permanent enthusiast. Their aim is simply to curb the excesses of behaviour if they start to interfere with the effectiveness of the meeting. And you need to accept this basic principle too. You can't turn a rabbiter into the briefest speaker at the table; they'll still be long-winded, but no longer painfully so. A domineering person isn't going to start sitting in the corner and avoiding geese for fear of having to say 'boo' to them. But they can be encouraged to tone down their behaviour so other people feel able to

Some people are a joy to attend meetings with – people like you (at least, once you've read this book)

express themselves without being shouted down or criticised – or simply unable to get a word in.

The principles

No matter what kind of person you are dealing with, the aim is to make things better, not worse. So whatever techniques you employ, the aim is to remove or reduce the problem behaviour without upsetting the person involved. There are two basic principles you should apply:

- **Don't get emotional.**
- **Be assertive.**

Staying calm

You are looking for a practical solution to the problem – a form of words or behaviour that achieves the desired effect. Look at it as a practical exercise, not an emotionally charged challenge. This can be tough when the problem behaviour generates an emotional response in you – sarcasm or put-downs, for example – but you won't get what you want any other way.

- **If people are using unpleasant behaviour deliberately, an emotional response tells them they're winning. They're getting a rise out of you. If you don't respond** emotionally, they're wasting their time and will be far more inclined to give up.

- If you allow yourself to show emotion you will undermine your own credibility, and the carefully prepared arguments you present will have less impact.
- People who cannot control their emotions are seen as weak, which is not the impression you want to give in front of your boss or other senior managers.

So keep telling yourself that the way to win is to remain calm and pleasant. You will retain the moral high ground, pull the rug out from under the feet of the person who is winding you up, and leave them looking foolish while you look smart. Now surely that's worth biting your tongue for?

thinking fast

HOLD YOUR PEACE

If you are too emotional to speak calmly to someone who is riling you, don't speak at all. Just breathe deeply while you count to 10. If it seems incumbent upon you to speak, ask the chairperson, 'Can we leave this for a moment until we've all calmed down a bit? I don't want things to get personal or unpleasant.' This, of course, puts you one up on the other person who presumably was quite happy to let things get unpleasant.

Assertiveness

Being assertive is all about treating other people as an equal, and expecting them to treat you as an equal. They may have a more senior rank than you, but they are equal as people and have no right to treat you as inferior in any way. There are three basic guidelines to being assertive.

- *Express your feelings*. An assertive person must be able to say how they feel, good or bad. You don't want to upset people, but you have rights too. If someone else is upsetting you or making you angry, say so. Don't be unpleasant or inflammatory about it, simply say, for example, 'I feel angry when you don't allow me to express my view.' If you start by saying 'I feel ... when you ...' you are far less likely to provoke conflict.

- *Be honest*. You are allowed to say what you think. From 'I disagree' to 'I have reservations about your idea; I think it needs reconsidering.' This means you can criticise people, but being honest means you must do it fairly. Don't just be rude.

- *Stand your ground*. Don't be intimidated into backing down. If you are put under pressure to change something you're not willing to change, simply keep repeating yourself, politely but firmly. If, for example, a colleague tries to persuade you to support their idea (which you actually think is dreadful) at a forthcoming meeting, just say, 'I'm sorry, I can't support it.' If they continue to insist, repeat 'I'm sorry, I'd like to be able to support it, but I can't.' Stand your ground and don't be bludgeoned.

THE DIFFICULT TYPES

While assertiveness and keeping calm are important techniques to use with all difficult people, certain types need specific handling. So here's a rundown of some of the more common difficult colleagues, and how to handle them in meetings. For more detailed advice on handling difficult types in general, have a look at *fast thinking: difficult people*.

The rabbiter

These people are infuriating, and it should be the chairperson's job to keep their contribution relatively brief. However, if they fail to do this, you can help do their job for them. The trick with these people is simple: don't try and stand in front of the car; just take over the wheel. So if Alex is wittering on about the logistics of an office move – and has either made the important points already or doesn't seem to be going to make any point at all – you can pick up on some remark and say, 'Actually, that's a really good point. And I've found some figures that back up just what Alex is saying …' and you've taken over the wheel.

Being assertive is all about treating other people as an equal, and expecting them to treat you as an equal

The pessimist

When someone says, 'It'll never work,' it's extremely frustrating as well as being unconstructive. On the other hand, the pessimists are often the ones who stop the group from making mistakes, and it may ease your frustration if you recognise this. You need to handle these people diplomatically, to avoid being seen to tread on the chairperson's toes.

> **When they express a negative view, ask them to make it specific: Why won't it work? Are they guessing or are they basing their assessment on the facts? Is it just a hunch or do they have previous experience of this sort of thing? Get them to be precise about which part of the project will create difficulties and why.**

thinking smart

GIVE THEM WHAT THEY WANT

Many rabbiters reiterate what they're saying over again because they're not convinced everyone's really got the point. So reassure them. Interrupt when they pause for breath and summarise what they're saying: 'So what you're saying is, if we started planning now we couldn't hope to move for at least 18 months?' The moment you get a word or gesture of assent, plough on before they get back into the flow: 'That's a good point. But won't it mean … ?'

- Ask them how they think the problem can be resolved. Again, get them to be specific; don't settle for 'I don't know – the whole thing looks like a waste of time to me.'

- Pessimists are often afraid of failure, and therefore avoid taking risks. They try to stop the whole meeting taking risks as well, by adopting such a negative viewpoint. Try asking them what they think the worst possible scenario could be as a result of following the course of action under discussion. This process often helps them to get their feelings in perspective.

The bully

You can't stop a bully completely if it's in their nature. But you can make sure that they don't bludgeon the meeting into becoming unpleasant or reaching frustrating or wrong decisions.

- Bullies usually pick on the weakest person around – often the youngest, least experienced member of the meeting. If this is you, you'll have to brush up on your assertiveness skills and learn to stand up for yourself. Don't try to fight back; simply refuse to back down.

- If someone else is being bullied, stand up for them. Don't be aggressive in their defence, or confrontational, but don't allow the domineering person to bully them. If they are trying to bludgeon them into agreeing a decision they clearly aren't happy with, come to their support and say, 'Actually, I think Peter has a valid point of view and he clearly believes it strongly. I don't

> The pessimists are often the ones who stop the group from making mistakes

think we should try to make him change his mind if he's unwilling' (note the diplomatic use of the word 'we' – you're not putting yourself in opposition to the bully).

- **Bullies tend to try and shout other people down. Don't react. If everyone else stays calm they will start to look rather silly losing their cool. They'll soon learn to stay in control rather than make a fool of themselves. This is a good example of how talking through the problem with sympathetic colleagues in advance of the meeting can help.**

The dominating type

These people don't bully, they simply take over so no one else can get a word in. They may be friendly and ebullient, or they may be prone to becoming aggressive if they think they're being silenced. The

thinking smart

STUCK RECORD

If someone is trying hard to bully you, adopt the stuck record technique. Just keep repeating the same point over and over. Don't get emotional or snappy, just repeat the same words each time they bully you, for example, 'I'm sorry, but I don't agree that this is the best option.' In a meeting this will make them look even more like a bully, while showing that you can be firm.

best person to control them is the chairperson, but if they're not doing their job properly you may have to lend a hand – without them feeling you're trying to take over, of course.

- Suggest – through the chairperson – that it might be helpful to go round the table and and let everyone take it in turn to give their views. This makes it far harder for the domineering type to take over.
- If someone else is unable to hold their own, help them out by saying, 'I'm very interested to hear what Paul has to say about this – didn't you deal with a similar issue at the last company you worked for?'
- If you're the one who can't get a word in, get together with a colleague who will ask for your contribution if you ask for theirs.
- Assertiveness will be important here, and try the old trick of saying, 'I've got three points I'd like to make …' (or however many it is, but try to limit it to a maximum of three). So long as you're reasonably brief, all but the most useless of chairpeople will make sure you're allowed to finish.

The put-down merchant

These people like to belittle others by making snide or sarcastic remarks, or ones which contain poorly concealed criticisms. Sadly, they can sometimes even be the chairperson. They are full of

> You can't stop a bully completely if it's in their nature. But you can make sure that they don't bludgeon the meeting

remarks such as, 'Late again, Kate? No surprises there,' or, 'You actually managed to read it, did you? Mind you, I don't imagine you understood much of it.' If it's any consolation, other people aren't likely to take the implications seriously, since they will all be well aware of the type of person they're coming from. But how do you deal with it?

- **The first thing is not to give them any ammunition. If you are always late, it's difficult to respond to the accusation, however unpleasantly they have chosen to put it. So make sure you give them no valid grounds for putting you down.**

- **If you rise to the bait, you will only create a row which will get you worse than nowhere, especially if the chairperson is the problem. If you rile this person, they'll get worse and not better.**

- **If you respond submissively, on the other hand, you encourage them to carry on putting down you and other people. If you are happy to ignore the remarks with dignity you can do so, but if you want them to stop this isn't the way to go about it.**

- **So you're left with the rational centre course – assertiveness. Reply with a polite question which challenges the put down. When they say, "Late again?" you reply "Apart from last Wednesday, when there was a tube strike, I don't believe I've been late for several months. Which occasion are you referring to?" This will**

take the wind out of their sails and you'll find, if you regularly employ this technique, they'll soon learn that if they try to belittle you it's them who will end up looking foolish.

Just remember that you can't change a person's character. Once you accept that, you stop expecting miracles and you find you're satisfied with a reasonable improvement. Once you have the basic techniques under your belt, difficult people suddenly don't seem nearly so difficult after all.

for next time

You will generally know the people you encounter at meetings. So you'll be aware that Jane will be at this afternoon's meeting and she's bound to be sarcastic, or Tom's going to be at the meeting tomorrow and that's likely to add 45 minutes to the running time. So plan your strategy in advance. You will probably have allies at the meeting too – other colleagues who are as aware as you are of these people's shortcomings. So get together and agree tactics which are amicable but effective.

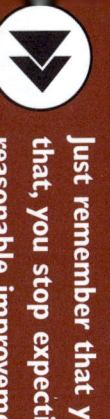

Just remember that you can't change a person's character. Once you accept that, you stop expecting miracles and you find you're satisfied with a reasonable improvement

5 chairperson problems

If you have a good, effective person in the chair at your meeting, you have a massive advantage. The meeting will run smoothly and to time, the atmosphere will be brisk but friendly, and everyone will have an equal chance to speak when they want to. In fact, the whole experience can be extremely pleasant, and the meeting will achieve what it sets out to.

But what if you don't have a skilled chairperson? Well, you have two options: put up with it, or change it. If you put up with it then everybody's time is wasted. Even if the meeting gets results they may not be the best ones, and they may take precious minutes or hours to achieve, which you simply can't spare. What's more, the process of reaching decisions and agreeing action points may entail unpleasantness and lead to rifts rather than unity among the members of the meeting.

If you decide to change things, you will in effect

have to take over part of the chairperson's job for them, or at least remind them how to do it properly. However, they may not take too kindly to your interference, so you'll have to be so subtle that they don't realise you're doing their job. There are plenty of different types of problem chairpeople – few of them (thankfully) are totally without skills. Some handle people badly, others are weak, some let meetings drag on, and so on.

We've already looked at how to cope with difficult people at the meeting when the chairperson fails to do it, and the next chapter will look at how to cope with conflict – again, even without back-up from your chairperson. So here are a few of the other classic problems that arise from bad chairing, and tips for limiting the damage.

THE MEETING OVERRUNS

There are few things more frustrating in this age of fast schedules and tight deadlines than strumming your fingers through long meetings which seem to be completely pointless, at least for you. But what can you do about it? To be honest, if you're not in the chair you're unlikely to make every meeting end on time, but there are still worthwhile techniques you can employ to speed things up.

> What if you don't have a skilled chairperson? Well, you have two options: put up with it, or change it

- We saw in the last chapter how to handle people who rabbit on – one of the big causes of wasted time at meetings. So if there's a witterer at your meeting, mug up on these techniques and use them plentifully if your chairperson doesn't.

- We also looked at influencing the agenda in advance in Chapter 2. Some meetings drag on more than they might because the agenda is planned poorly. If the result of item 6 influences the decision made at item 2, the meeting may have to go back and discuss item 2 all over again. If you know your chairperson is inclined to issue such agendas, read the agenda carefully as soon as it arrives and look for this kind of logical flaw. If you spot any problems, speak to the chairperson and tactfully suggest that it might be more practical to discuss the items in a different order.

thinking smart

HERE'S ONE I PREPARED EARLIER ...

Sometimes you can see that a certain agenda item is only relevant to a few of the people at the meeting. If you're one of them, talk to the others and then contact the chairperson, offering to hold a mini-meeting in advance. That way instead of discussing the item – with everyone else throwing in their twopenny worth because they're there – you can simply present your results to the main meeting and move on to the next item.

> One of the big delays to many meetings is that the group reaches an agreement but then continues the discussion without appearing to recognise the fact. The meeting ceases to be useful, and turns into some kind of group therapy session instead. The solution is simple. If the chairperson isn't doing their job, you'll have to do it for them. Be deferential so as not to put any backs up, and say to the chairperson: 'Am I right in thinking that we're all agreed on this?'

> One of your options is to try to get out of part of the meeting. Ask the chairperson in advance if they can re-order the items on the agenda so you can leave part way through, having been present for all the items you need to contribute to. You'll have to generate a pretty good excuse, or everyone will soon be doing it with this kind of long-winded chairperson. But if you can arrange a meeting with an important client, for example, you'll have a good excuse.

thinking smart

DON'T BE LATE

One tip if you're aiming to leave a meeting early: arrive on time. It means you won't have resentment built up against you already when you leave, and you'll look less like someone unorganised and more like someone with a genuine reason for leaving before the end.

If you're not in the chair you're unlikely to make every meeting end on time, but there are still worthwhile techniques you can employ to speed things up

THE DISCUSSION ISN'T KEPT UNDER CONTROL

Some chairpeople simply can't seem to keep on top of the discussion. Either they allow endless digressions while people wander off the point, or they allow endless disagreements without directing the debate towards a conclusion of some kind. Either way, you're stuck in a meeting that's going nowhere, wishing *you* could go anywhere but here.

Your best bet as far as digressions are concerned is to try to speed things up through the chairperson (underlining, rather than undermining, the fact that they are in charge). Comments such as, 'I wonder if this is really relevant?' or 'Surely we all know the facts; shouldn't we be discussing their implications?' should jolt the chairperson into doing their job a little more effectively.

Another option, especially where disagreement is rife, is to suggest to the chairperson that it might help if the relevant people set up a separate meeting to discuss the issue and report back next time, rather than waste the meeting's time now. If you're involved, offer to organise it yourself; that way you may well be able to end up chairing it, and you can make sure it runs effectively.

thinkingfast

NON-STARTERS

Some items can never reach the conclusion they are supposed to because vital facts are missing, relevant people are missing, or the conclusion depends on another decision that hasn't been made yet. A good chairperson will identify these non-starters fast, and abandon the item. But if they don't, you can point it out to them: 'Is there any point discussing this without Ali? Don't we need his input to make a decision?'

DECISIONS ARE RUSHED

Some chairpeople share your view that meetings should not be places to waste time. They feel it so strongly that they are inclined to rush through the agenda, often without allowing everyone sufficient time to contribute. In fact, they are defeating their own object – by not allowing enough time for debate they are at risk of missing vital facts and reaching wrong decisions. All of which render the meeting a waste of time.

But what can you do about it? For a start, you can learn to be brief and succinct, as we saw earlier. The people who really miss out with this approach are

---

Another option, especially where disagreement is rife, is to suggest to the chairperson that it might help if the relevant people set up a separate meeting

the wafflers. And you can also contact the chairperson in advance about really important issues and ask for five minutes on item 5, or whatever it is you need. Once they've agreed to it in advance, they are far more likely to honour that agreement. And you have to do your share by sticking to the time you've asked for (if you're even quicker, they're more likely to agree again next time).

If your chairperson is determined to rush the meeting despite your best efforts, there is little you can ultimately do. But at least you can insist that your views are recorded on the minutes. Ask for the minutes to state that you feel the issue has not been discussed sufficiently.

THE CHAIRPERSON CONTROLS ALL THE DECISIONS

It is extremely frustrating coping with meetings where the chairperson is domineering. But it happens. They control the discussions and the decisions, and the rest of you wonder what the point is of your being there at all. Unfortunately, the chairperson is holding all the cards, and you have little room for manoeuvre.

Once again, your best bet is at least to insist (politely of course) that your disagreement with any decisions be recorded in the minutes. The minutes are a vital document and can be referred to later, so you will be able to distance yourself from any dreadful decisions in future if you need to by pointing out that your disagreement was recorded at the time.

If you can get enough support for this approach among your colleagues, your chairperson will find the minutes frequently record several names of those who have disagreed with them. It may not have any influence on their style (such people aren't known for their searing self-appraisal skills), but it has as much chance as anything of drawing their attention to the fact that they are autocratic and domineering.

> By not allowing enough time for debate they are at risk of missing vital facts and reaching wrong decisions

for next time

The best way to cope with poor chairing is to become a surrogate chairperson yourself – without the real chairperson noticing, of course. The more chairing skills you can learn, the better equipped you'll be to do this. And chairing skills are always going to be a useful skill to have under your belt.

So take every opportunity to learn how the professionals do it, and put yourself forward to chair meetings and get hands-on practice if you can. This may be at work, or it may be with some group or charity you belong to outside work (they're the toughest to chair, I can tell you, because you don't actually have any authority over the members of the meeting; you can't sack them or even discipline them).

You may also find it useful to read one of the other books in this series all about chairing skills, *fast thinking: team meeting*.

▼ You will be able to distance yourself from any dreadful decisions in future if you need to by pointing out that your disagreement was recorded at the time

6 coping with conflict

Weak chairpeople, colleagues who take a negative view of everything, meetings that go on for hours ... all these frustrations can seem nothing compared with finding yourself in a meeting which seems to be more of a battleground than a place of healthy debate.

One of the reasons that many meetings turn into battles is because of the hidden agenda that's behind the one you have on the table in front of you. Many – perhaps all – the other people at the meeting are competing with each other for status, territory and ultimately promotion. Healthy competition has turned into unhealthy point-scoring, and what should be a forum for discussion has turned into an arena for fighting and back-stabbing.

THE CAUSES OF CONFLICT

There are two basic conflicts going on in most meetings of this kind:

- *Status battles*: whoever can prove themselves most senior reckons to be first in line for the next promotion. So everyone wants it to be their proposals which get agreed, and *their* arguments which win the day. All of this will make them appear more important than their colleagues.
- *Turf wars*: each manager has their own territory or department. And woe betide anyone who presumes to know more about production than the production manager, or attempts to take a prestigious project away from PR and get sales to run it instead. No one is prepared to give an inch of their territory, since the size and power of their department defines their personal clout.

And *your* problem is to find a way of crossing the battleground without ever having to take up arms. You see, these fighters are quite right. Meetings are a great place to flex your muscles and lay the groundwork for future successes. If you opt out of the fight entirely and surrender whenever you're challenged, you're not going to win that next promotion.

On the other hand, if you join in and the temperature rises, not only do you risk looking petty alongside the others (rather than rising above the conflict), but the meeting itself will suffer. It will become hard, or even impossible, for it to

> One of the reasons that many meetings turn into battles is because of the hidden agenda that's behind the one you have on the table in front of you

achieve the results it sets out to, and that's in no one's interest. If you go head-to-head with one of your key rivals, you have far less chance of getting them to agree to your ideas than if you can get them on your side.

So what you need to know is: How can you keep the temperature down and the atmosphere good humoured, without giving any ground yourself? Well, here's the fast thinker's guide to coping with conflict.

STATUS BATTLES

Your opponents at the meeting want their ideas to win against yours because they see this as an indication that they are superior to you. This is why many people employ underhand techniques or become angry and emotional when they see they are in danger of losing a particular argument.

We'll be looking at how to handle anger specifically in a moment, but broadly speaking your aim should be to win the argument – obviously – but do it in a way that makes them feel as positive and successful as possible. After all, you can afford to be generous over the details if you've won the battle.

thinking smart

> **SPOT CHECK**
>
> As far as your own status is concerned, you will do best if you are seen to be calm, rational and amicable (as well as expressing well-reasoned arguments supported by well-prepared facts). So check up on yourself from time to time by asking, 'Am I doing myself harm or good by this behaviour?'

Be pleasant

For a start, be as pleasant and friendly as you can, and ignore any attempts to goad you with criticisms or personal put-downs. You will only rile your opponent if you are arrogant, sarcastic or smug. The nicer you are, the less they will mind losing to you and the less they will therefore fight the status battle alongside the practical argument you're debating.

Practise win/win negotiating

Win/win negotiating, as you may know, is the art of winning a negotiation in such a way that the other side feels they have also won. Give them as many brownie points as you can (while standing firm on the core issue), so they come away feeling like a winner and not a loser. So, for example:

- **Give them plenty of credit and praise** – 'These figures Alex has come up with really are invaluable ...' or, 'I think the reason this solution will work is because Alex has such a strong team to carry it out ...'

- **Make any minor concessions you can** – 'I'm still certain that this is the right way to go. But I think Alex is right about delaying until after the summer ...'

- **Refer back to their previous successes** – 'It's certainly possible to organise a project this size in the time if we had to. Look at the new computer system we put in last year; Alex's team organised that in only four months, and it went without a hitch.'

Any other business

We touched on this earlier, and saw how your best bet is to prepare for topics which might be sprung on you under any other business in order to catch you on the hop. If you are ready for it, this is the best way to deal with the 'aob' trick. Your opponent is the one who'll be caught on the hop, not you, when you respond with carefully researched facts and figures and well-prepared arguments. You can turn the tables on them nicely.

But suppose you really aren't ready for it, or simply never saw it coming? In that case you need to convince the chairperson that the item must be delayed until the next meeting. Don't whinge, like a child, 'Thats's not fair' (although it isn't). Point out that it will compromise the meeting. Explain that you weren't expecting this item to come up, and you need time to prepare so you can bring relevant and useful data to the meeting.

One useful technique here is to point out not only that you need to do essential research for this item (and give an example or two), but also that you want to talk to other people. This seems to broaden the field of missing information if the topic is taken now, and shows that it is not just a personal preference to save this item for later, but one which affects other people too. You have an excellent chance of delaying the item with a remark like, 'If I'd known this item was coming up I'd have talked to my deliveries manager about the logistics of introducing a fast-track service.'

thinking smart

ROUND TWO

Your opponent may well argue that this item can't wait until the next meeting. If you can't persuade the meeting otherwise, suggest organising a separate meeting in a few days' time – after you've done your research – so it can still be discussed before the deadline your opponent is arguing for. That should take the wind out of their sails.

> Your opponents at the meeting want their ideas to win against yours because they see this as an indication that they are superior to you

TURF WARS

You're in big trouble if you tread on other people's toes in a meeting. Your colleagues no more want to share their expertise with you than Henry V wanted to share Normandy with the French. They are as likely to give up part of their responsibilities to you as Margaret Thatcher was to give up the Falklands to Argentina. People are naturally territorial, and you forget it at your peril.

So don't even think about putting forward ideas which entail reducing someone's reponsibilities unless you either:

1. **Suggest replacing them with other responsibilities (preferably ones which seem more prestigious)**

or

2. **Suggest that they are too important to do them, for example, 'If we handled the day-to-day paperwork for Mike, that would free up his team for more important tasks such as high-level negotiations with customers.'**

Taking responsibilities away from people isn't the only way you can tread on their toes. No one likes it if you give the impression that you know more about their department or their area of expertise than they do. So don't make bald statements about other people's territories. Instead of saying, '92 per cent of our orders are repeat business,' ask the sales manager, 'Joe, what percentage of our orders are repeat business?' or, 'Mike, am I right in thinking that … ?'

DEALING WITH ANGER

I had a school-friend whose father was a vicar. Mike was once leafing through the manuscript of one of his father's sermons, which had notes in the margin. He was highly amused to find that his

thinking fast

ASK AWAY

Asking questions of your opponents is a very handy technique, and one you'll need if you've cut things fine in the preparation department. If you want to disagree with someone but haven't researched the facts to back up your case, don't disagree openly. Just ask them questions: 'What percentage of our orders are repeat business?' or, 'How would this proposal work when we're short staffed?' or, 'We tried a similar approach with the Jakeson contract. How did that work out in terms of cash flow?' You're effectively doing your research in the meeting and, since you're not disagreeing with anyone, tempers won't get frayed.

You're in big trouble if you tread on other people's toes in a meeting. Your colleagues no more want to share their expertise with you than Henry V wanted to share Normandy with the French

father had written himself a note at one point which read, 'Shout here, argument weak'.

In fact, his father had registered an important technique, and one which many people use at meetings. They use force of personality because they haven't got force of argument. How often do people get emotional and angry when they have all the arguments on their side and they know they're going to win? They don't need to. So as soon as anyone starts to get angry, you know you've got them on the run.

Nevertheless, you don't actually want a colleague who spits blood at you. You will be far more popular with the meeting as a whole – and look far more like a good promotion prospect to your bosses – if you can keep the proceedings calm and pleasant as you politely win the battle.

And the technique for doing this is very simple. You remain calm yourself, don't respond with emotion, but simply pick out the facts of what is being said and deal with those as you would if the person were talking clamly. If they keep haranguing you, just wait patiently until they run out of steam before you reply. A half-decent chairperson should intervene to let you speak but, if they don't, appeal to them by saying, calmly and politely, 'May I respond to that point?'

thinking smart

GO ON – HAVE A LAUGH

Laughter is a great way to create a feeling of unity in a meeting, and if you can do it an injection of humour can dispel any unpleasantness that is building up. The only rule is, don't make a joke at the expense of anyone in the meeting (or any of their close allies). The only exception to this is that you can always make jokes against yourself.

This might sound as though your opponent will get to do all the talking and you will be unable to put your case. But in fact it doesn't tend to work like that. Not only will they look very silly if they're the only one losing control of their emotions, but they're not likely to keep it up for very long if they don't get a heated response from you. They will burn out fast (after a brief period where you look cool and reasonable while they look like a three-year-old child), and the discussion will become calmer. You'll need to use all the skills we've already covered to keep them calm, but you can do it and it will be worth it.

No one likes it if you give the impression that you know more about their department or their area of expertise than they do

◀◀ for next time

Think through in advance whether any of your ideas or proposals will be seen to damage someone else's status, or trespass on their territory. If so, think through ways of presenting them so these effects are removed or at least moderated. Find concessions you can make, or compensating factors to bring out to show that the other person's status or territory isn't damaged. You can talk through these ideas with colleagues who support your ideas.

As soon as anyone starts to get angry, you know you've got them on the run

7 types of meeting

All the guidelines we've covered so far are relevant to any meeting you attend. The only exceptions to this are team briefings (where you don't have to contribute at all), and meetings with about 40 or 50 people or more, which are more like presentations with an opportunity to ask questions. But for any other type of meeting the techniques you've just learnt will see you right.

There are, however, different types of meeting and it's worth looking briefly at the main types because particular techniques will come to the fore in each. So here's a rundown of some of the more specific skills you'll need for:

- **departmental meetings**
- **inter-departmental meetings**
- **project meetings**
- **external meetings.**

Departmental meetings

Hopefully, your department is pretty well united as a group, and turf wars are less of a problem. However, competition to be seen as a hot prospect by the boss can be strong in this kind of meeting, so conflict can be rife. It is particularly worth avoiding conflict within the department since you all have to work together closely, and there is a strong, everyday need for a sense of unity. Anything you can do to promote group bonding will be appreciated by everyone (including your boss):

- **Be a peacemaker, and use all your skills to avoid conflict with your colleagues.**
- **Use humour. It bonds a group faster than anything else, and will help others to see you as a natural leader, and someone who brings people together.**

Departmental meetings naturally involve people who know each other well, so you'll find that any regular techniques you use will have to be fairly subtle or your colleagues will have your number pretty quickly. Ruses such as dotting reports you haven't actually read with post-it notes to look as if you've gone through them (suggested in Chapter 2), will be seen through fairly swiftly in this kind of

> Anything you can do to promote group bonding will be appreciated by everyone (including your boss)

meeting. And here are a couple more guidelines for departmental meetings:

- **They can get long-winded, so make sure you're not a part of the problem. Keep your contributions brief. And look for opportunities to suggest that sub-groups get together to solve things and report back, rather than waste the meeting's time now.**

- **Since you know the chairperson well – who is presumably your boss – and you know the format and style of the meetings, you have a better chance than usual to influence the agenda. So get in early with your suggestions and ideas as we discussed in Chapter 2.**

INTER-DEPARTMENTAL MEETINGS

This is where the turf wars can really turn nasty. So your key focus here should be to use the

thinking smart

A PROBLEM SHARED

There are plenty of opportunities at departmental meetings to talk to colleagues in advance and rally support for your particular cause, perhaps in exchange for supporting them on another item. So look through the agenda and see where a joint effort would make more sense than going solo.

techniques we've covered for avoiding trespassing on others' territories. If you want to disagree diplomatically, do it by asking questions rather than by challenging outright. Pre-meeting diplomacy can be effective, too, in spotting and avoiding this kind of trouble.

In both departmental and project meetings, the general idea is that everyone in the meeting is working together towards a joint objective. But inter-departmental meetings are a very different thing. They often become negotiations in which you are trying to push an idea through or get a proposal stopped, in opposition to others at the meeting. So you will need well-researched and well-prepared arguments for any agenda item that you want to influence the outcome of.

In order to keep the peace in this potentially explosive atmosphere, it helps to take notes of any relevant remarks and refer back to them. Write down the name of the person who made the comment, so you can praise people regularly by saying 'Eileen's comment earlier about the need to get it right first time was spot on. Which is why I think it's so vital that we ...' The more people you can indicate unity with, the better.

11 thinking fast

DON'T PUT YOURSELF IN THE LINE OF FIRE

We've already looked at how to cope with an emotional or angry opponent. But don't fall into the trap of dealing with it if you don't have to. If other people are slugging it out across the table, don't stick in your twopenny worth – just keep your head down until the hostile fire has passed.

Project meetings

These tend to be cooperative, productive meetings since everyone knows they are working towards a joint goal. Turf wars are rare, and even status battles tend to be reserved for other meetings. The biggest danger with project meetings is that time will be wasted by being unclear about action points.

Project meeting minutes are packed with action points – that's what the meetings are for. The chairperson should make sure that priorities, budgets and deadlines are all crystal clear, but often they fail to do this as meticulously as they should. When this happens you need to take over, at least on any action point that concerns you in any way. So keep asking questions to clarify the action points, such as:

- **Who is actually doing this task? Am I doing all of it, or is Alan organising the transport?**
- **When is the deadline for this? Is that for the outline agreement, or for the final decision?**
- **Should I let Tariq know when we've completed this stage, or will he go ahead at the end of the month regardless?**

External meetings

These might be meetings with other companies, meetings you attend as a member of a voluntary organisation or charity, or meetings of trade association representatives. They are less of an arena for status contests than most meetings (no complaints there) since there isn't usually anyone to impress who is in a position to promote any of the people at the meeting. Nevertheless, you are presumably there because you want to influence some course of action, so there are still arguments to be won.

> The biggest danger with project meetings is that time will be wasted by being unclear about action points

- The most significant point about this kind of meeting is that you probably don't know everyone there, or at least don't know them well. So you may not be sure what their attitudes are and what areas they may be touchy about or feel they are the acknowledged authority on. Consequently, your best bet is to speak as late as possible, after you've had a chance to listen to the other contributions, so you can better gauge the response you'll get.

- The exception to this is if you want to direct the discussion from the start to make sure everyone is focused on what you see as the key aspect of the issue. You may want to speak early if you want to say, for example, 'I think it's important to be clear that our real objective should be to block this legislation ...', or 'I want to emphasise that the key question we need to answer is, "Can we afford this?"'

- When you speak, it is particularly helpful at this kind of meeting to summarise the issue before contributing, especially highlighting – briefly – those points you want to support or oppose.

- If you are attending a meeting of some voluntary body, it's worth noting that these are often chaired by amateurs with poor chairing skills. It would be well worth reviewing Chapter 5, since you may need to diplomatically do part of the chairperson's job for them.

for next time

Take some time before your next important meeting to think through the type of meeting it is, and to prepare yourself for the particular skills you'll need. Remind yourself of the key behaviours to avoid or to use in order to be both a peacekeeper *and* be effective in getting what you want.

Take some time before your next important meeting to think through the type of meeting it is

going to a meeting in 15 minutes

Cutting it a bit fine, aren't we? If the meeting's important, you're going to have to think very smart to have your act together a quarter of an hour from now. The aim is not only to be prepared, but also to come across well, impress everyone at the meeting and win any arguments which are important to you. So let's get cracking on the sprint version of preparing for meetings.

- Look through the agenda and decide which are the most important items for you. There may be only one, or there may be two or three. I just hope at this short notice that there aren't any more than that.

- Decide what your objective is for each of these items (have a quick look at Chapter 1). Are you trying to get a point agreed, defer a decision, or defeat a proposal?

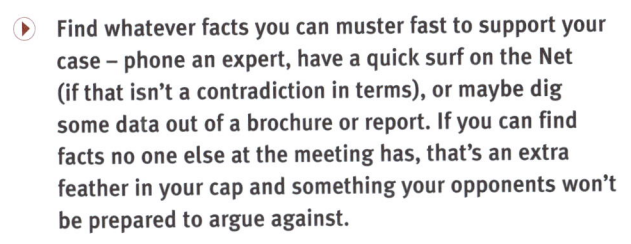

- List the key two or three arguments in favour of your view, and the key ones your opponents will put that you'll need to defeat.

- Find whatever facts you can muster fast to support your case – phone an expert, have a quick surf on the Net (if that isn't a contradiction in terms), or maybe dig some data out of a brochure or report. If you can find facts no one else at the meeting has, that's an extra feather in your cap and something your opponents won't be prepared to argue against.

- On no account be tempted to make up data (and it can be tempting when you're in a hurry). You may get away with it 20 times in a row, but when you finally get caught it will undermine the credibility of every valid fact you ever present at any other meeting.

- Prepare a mini-presentation – as little as three or four sentences – for each item you've decided is really important to you (see page 35).

- If you want to challenge other people in the meeting and you don't have the facts to do it, remember that you can challenge them by asking questions (see page 75) rather than by disagreeing directly.

I hope you've got the adrenaline to cope with all that succesfully. But however well you get away with it this time, try to leave yourself longer in

> The aim is not only to be prepared, but also to come across well, impress everyone at the meeting and win any arguments which are important to you

future and you'll find you can make the extra time you put in earn its keep in terms of the results you get back out. And isn't it great when meetings feel worthwhile and achieve what you want?